With very best wishes

Bob

10/20/2016

THE RUEFUL HIPPOPOTAMUS

THE RUEFUL HIPPOPOTAMUS

&

Other Light Verse

ROBERT HANROTT

B|Y|D
PRESS

Library of Congress Control Number: 2016905626

ISBN 978-0-9721035-1-0

1424 33rd Street NW
Washington, DC 20007

For information, contact: rhanrott@rcn.com

*Dedicated to the memory of my Father,
Charles Hanrott (1911–1989)*

*For Henry, Jemima, Wynn,
Lara, and Trea Hanrott,
and for those who come after them*

and

*With grateful thanks
to Martha for her advice*

Contents

WHIMSY

The Rueful Hippopotamus

Research now seems to indicate
That hippos can communicate,
Like dolphins or the great blue whale,
With clicks. And thereby hangs a tale,
For they can hear beneath the water
Things on land they didn't oughta,
And from the bank can hear what's said
By sweethearts on the river bed.

Imagine you're a great bull hippo,
Flumping down to take a dip-oh
In the greasy, grey Limpopo
With the girls in your seraglio.
You've had a hot and tiresome day
Chasing other males away.
You've gored them, left them sore and bleeding;
Now you are intent on breeding.

You've had your fill of the savannah.
You're young, you're fit, you're top banana.
Why, every female hippolump
With big brown eyes and handsome rump
Is sure to swoon and yearn to be
The mother of your family.
Ah! Potty, with inviting lips;
And Mussy, with the sexy hips;

Heffy, with her nostrils flaring;
Lumpie, her whole midriff baring!
Yes, all will find you simply stunning.
Just one word and they'll come running!
With thundering and galumphing stride,
You trundle to the riverside.
But nowhere, nowhere can you spy
Your eager hippopotamae.

And then to your acute dismay
You hear an amorata say,
Oh, dearie me, oh, what a shocker,
Straight from Davey Jones's locker,
Deep below the surface swirl:
"He don't know how to treat a girl.
I don't expect no chocs or flowers,
Or sweet-talk that will last for hours.

"But when in heat and I'm his squeeze,
I wish he'd simply add a 'please?'"
"I quite agree." (another voice)
"I wish we girls could have a choice.
He's rude and gruff and rather rough,
And isn't even good at stuff.
He'd like to think he's quite a stud;
I'd much prefer to doze in mud."

(A third voice) "Yes, he's humourless and brusque
And far too quick to use a tusk.
I too agree with both of you.
My preference is for a zoo.
At least in zoos you laze away
With three square, well-cooked meals a day.

And if you have to mate, o.k.,
You do it on a Saturday
With hordes of visitors in sight.
They keep a hippo male polite."

You're shocked, you're shattered, angry too.
Was this gossip aimed at you?
Such comments make a chap's skin crawl.
You never fancied them at all!
And lest you lose your pride and face,
You move off to another place,
Flumping down to take a dip-oh
In the greasy, grey Limpopo.

The Well-Dressed Fox

A fox without his shoes and socks
Is incorrectly dressed;
His jacket should be laundered
And his trousers should be pressed.
For, hunting in the woodland,
He might meet a deer or vole,
A marmoset or hedgehog,
A tortoise or a mole.
Imagine his embarrassment should
Such a thing occur.
And he passed by and said, "Good day,"
In just his under-fur.

The Angry Tree

"What have I done to deserve it?"
Asked the maple tree to the yew.
"I have quietly grown in their garden,
Causing no complaint hitherto.
I have given a great deal of pleasure,
And have offered them summertime shade.
I am still fit and spry as the seasons go by,
As I enter my eightieth decade.

"Of a sudden my owners are anguished:
'The foundations will break up and crumble.
The roots when it rains will be blocking the drains,
And the house? It will totter and tumble.
This tree is upending the patio,
And look at that brickwork, that wall!
I am suffering pangs. Why, that branch overhangs
The next garden. I dread lest it fall.'

"But isn't this usual with humans?
For years they will gladly enjoy you.
But one seed of doubt and they'll panic about,
And find any excuse to destroy you.
They've given me such cramped conditions.
I have suffered a tinge of neglect.
But respecting their space, I have lessened the pace
Of the natural growth you'd expect.

"I admit I shed leaves in the autumn,
And other detritus all year.
It is true I'm unable with no stainless steel cable
To keep my arms up in the air.
I agree I have caused minor damage,
That my roots have been causing alarm.
But really they oughta have given me water
And I'd never have done any harm.

"I ask you, who made the decision
To plant me so near to their dwelling?
It's fair to proclaim that they too are to blame.
It's them, and not I, who need felling.
I'm proposing a counter-injunction;
Their death sentence clearly needs dodging.
I'll insist it's not me who should soon cease to be.
Rather, they should demolish their lodging!"

The Rhyme

Poets now despise the rhyme,
Or that's the affectation.
But nonsense is as nonsense does,
And what is worse
Than bad blank verse?
Gibberish strung upon a line,
Conforming to the fashion?
The wish being father to the thought,
It's promptly
Found
To be
Profound.

Rhymes outdated? That's just rot!
Some can rhyme, and some can not.

It's content, not the form, that counts,
And mastery of meaning.
A certain discipline of mind
Is requisite when using rhyme.
So don't reject the tools at hand,
Misused as they may be.
The means can justify the end.
My point is penned.
Enough!
The End!

The Tune

The Tune, just like its friend, the Rhyme,
Has had its era and its time.
Rodgers, Hart and Hammerstein
Now seem as quaint as Auld Lang Syne.
And big bands that were once the rage,
Are relics of a bygone age.

A booming sound in deep bass clef
Now satisfies the future deaf.
The "melody" that kids applaud
Is eight bars on a single chord;
The words, however subtle, drowned
In thumping, unrelenting sound.

Juries now give ecstatic votes
To songs strung out on single notes.
Am I too old, perhaps ungallant,
If I suggest a lack of talent?
Can the young recall or croon
A modern song without a tune?

Could it be composers now
Would write a tune, but don't know how?

The Comma

I'd like to take a bomber
And obliterate the comma,
Whose phrase attenuation
Is the bane of punctuation.
I always use too many;
In my prose they're ten a penny;
While lawyers, rather direly,
Have abolished them entirely.

A comma alters, meaning
Is the goal to which I'm leaning.
The comma's like a word or tense—
Change it and you change the sense.
Omit it and you must work out
What the prose is all about.

But I am truly disconcerted
When the comma is inverted.
Use the single or the double?
Bound to get you into trouble.
To place quote marks within quotations
Can cause a war between two nations.
It's all a little much for me.

And so I'll let the reader pout
And grimace, and just sort it out.

Silver, Orange, Purple, Month

I have been told that the words silver, orange, purple and month are impossible to rhyme. Here is my attempt to rhyme them.

When you meet
A foreigner,
Defer and always
Try to honour her.
She might be shy,
Small as a wisp,
Or sometimes have
A painful lisp.
Furthermore,
Although your better,
She may have trouble
With a letter.

What we call orange
She calls *olange*
Discussing *thilver*
She means silver,
The word purple
Comes out *burple*.

You could speak thus
In just a month,

Meet frequently
And not just wunth.
Now the linguithtic
Die is catht,
Repeat this verth
But twyth ath fatht.

Now You Are Five

Now you've reached the age of five
We hope you've time to play.
To sit upon your bed alone
And dream some time away.

Imagine you've gone back in time
Ten million years ago—
Watching dinosaurs stroll by,
Grazing as they go.
Volcanoes spouting fire and rock,
The sun a misty speck,
You ride a brontosaurus
With your arms around his neck.

You're traveling in the desert
In the hot, hot heat—
Sitting on a camel
With its big, fat feet.
It's funny on a camel,
They just munch, munch, munch,
Which is really rather odd because
They don't have lunch.

Imagine you're a driver
Of a car with massive power—
Speeding round a circuit

At two hundred miles an hour,
Weaving past the slower cars,
Shooting round the bends,
Acknowledging the cheering
As the big race ends.

Imagine you've an eagle eye
You're master of the ball—
A world-class, famous golfing pro
The finest of them all.
Imagine you're a sailor
Upon the stormy sea,
Or traveling in a rocket
To a far-off galaxy.

Imagine you're a pianist
The greatest of the age—
Playing music you composed
Alone upon the stage.
You play the music perfectly;
The audience stands because
They adore you, and they thank you
With their thunderous applause.

You will find when you're grown up
True adventures of all kinds;
But nothing beats daydreaming
And adventures of the mind.

When God Lost the Planet

Each day unfurled
Another world!
God sits up there and gently nurses
Spanking, brand new universes.

Purblinding flash!
Oh, boom and crash!
A zillion atoms spun in space.
Where did they fly? Some place, some place.

For thirteen billion years, we're told,
Did God his galaxies unfold
With neutron stars and cosmic rays.
Thus did God spend timeless days.

For goodness' sake,
One needs a break.
Even those with mighty power
Like to relax for half an hour.

He thinks a thought!
Just what he sought
To liven up the daily grind—
He has a unique scheme in mind!

Aha! Ambition!
Matchless mission—

A scheme to create a race of men
With ethics and with acumen!

Experiment
Was his intent.
"I'll pick a rock of random worth,
And, ah! I'll call the planet 'Earth'!

"And at its birth
I'll make this Earth
As beauteous as an April sonnet
And place my new creations on it.

"They'll look like me,
Be good like me,
And every man will love his wife,
And thank me for his daily life!"

And so it was, and in a trice
God created paradise,
And placed in it a married pair,
A test to see how they would fare.

But space expands
If left unplanned.
A planet whirls away in space,
And nothing's left to fill its place.

Space grew too vast,
And God at last,
Taking years to get around,
Discovered Earth could not be found.

Thus men are left
On Earth, bereft,
Without a God to tell them "nay,"
Lost amidst the Milky Way.

It's rather rare
To sit up there,
And even in ten billion years,
To lose a planet in the spheres.

"Oh, huge mistake
For me to make!
Where is that H_2O and granite?
Where is my chosen little planet?

"Oh! Fractured hope!
How will they cope,
Lost in the vast ethereal sphere
Gripped by suspicion, greed and fear?

"Oh, doom, oh, gloom.
Not I? Then whom?
Who will be there to keep them moral,
To teach them how to love, not quarrel?"

God searches here,
He searches there,
On moons, black dwarfs, dark energy,
But not a human could He see.

"Ah! Infinitesimal speck!
Hey, what the heck?

If men on Earth possess a flaw
Forget it! I'll just make some more."

And thus time passed
Until at last,
While rambling through a group of stars,
Why, Earth appeared, alongside Mars.

Ah! Eureka!
Planet seeker!
He cried, "Aha, that's where they've gone!
Let's see how they are getting on."

Amazed, He found his two creations
Had spawned a multitude of nations.
No one thought or spoke the same,
Or, if in the wrong, would take the blame.

"Jehovah! Lord!
(With one accord!)
We're glad you've come as prophesied!
We thought we'd see you when we died."

So saying, men
Proceeded then
To pepper God like proper pests
With thousands of inane requests.

Most were self-seeking,
Falsehood-reeking,
"Bless me, Lord, and kindly strike
And punish those whom I dislike."

"Oh, God, to whom we genuflect
Mine's by far the holiest sect.
We praise you more, and they are weird.
What's more, we wear a longer beard."

And God was pained
When people claimed
He'd picked upon a chosen few
And helped them win a war or two.

And God above
Said "Where is love?
I should have been around to ground 'em,
I rather wish I'd never found 'em."

EVERYDAY LIFE

The Georgetowne House Toure

As Experienced by an Olde Englisheman, with apologies to
Chaucer, Milton, Dryden, whoever . . .

Wen ye month of Aprylle turns its Course,
Then house-bounde wimmin comme out in force,
Enjoy the birdyes and the freshe Springe aire
That in their Citye is so pure and clare.
They folde their Pullovers and winter Smockes,
And don their Sneakers and forego their Sockes.
With back-packes, visors, and reluctant Spouses,
They set off to examine Rich Men's Houses.
No Grand Tour has such profound allure
As Georgetowne's Olde, renownèd Springe House Toure.

To snoop, to prye, to gape, and jealously to stare
Is alle Creation's Nature everywhere.
Plato somewhere must have mentioned it,
And Shakespeare too, although he rote with wit.
Noseynesse goes backe unto the Arc,
Attested to by Ovid and Petrarch.
When Beastes in the Arc had reached their limit,
They promptly, curious, nosed about within it.
Male gods on Mount Olympus poked all day
Round Aphrodite's lodgings, when away.

In Horace, Virgil, Seneca, you'll find
Evidence of an Enquiringe Minde:
Read them with Care that verily you may Spotte
What the Wealthiest have that you do not.
Is it their Taste, or that of a Designer?
That Rugge, Hand-made or mass-produced in China?
That *Personality* with famous name,
They ache to ape him and to buy the same.
Lives of Rich and Famous cause such chatter;
But how they maketh money doth not matter.

Thus am I present, shepherding the Flocke,
In a Butler's Pantry, chock-a-block
With Touristes, mostly wimmin, sticky-beaking.
Now down the old Dumb-waiter they are peeking,
While I'm explaining how in Olden Times
Little Children charged with Household Crimes
In that Contrapcioun would be whisked away.
Up? Down? Who cares? Please have a pleasant day!
But Levity is seldom understood;
If the Owner's rich then surely he is Good.

First comes a Ladye, up she roundly spoke:
"Those cupboards are all Olde and made of Oak,
While they are all well made, they are too High."
Which was my cue to telle her frankly why
The owners of this famous, grande olde Mansion
Had undergone a recent Great Expansion.
They were two sliteley-builded newlyweds
Who couldn't reach the Shelves above their Heads.
'Tis said the couple have for Months been itchin'
To build a brand new, modern Kitchen.

"This bane a wee cookery for the size of Hoose!"
The Ladye saith (I've rendered her quite loose).
"Yes," saith I, "designèd by a Manne
To keep his wife confined with Frying Pan.
All accoutrements are there for cooking,
And Sauce Pans handy without even looking.
Wi' never an inch to fit in an Assistant,
The risk of being asked to help was distant.
Asked to chop an onion he could thus reply,
'I cannot fit. If fitting, both would cry.'"

So off the Visitors go, with zeale, intent,
Repeating Faery Tales I did invent.
Filled with ideas for Chaires and Lampes and Shades
And Papery Patternes and Fine Brocades,
Copious Storage and sufficient Drawers,
Of Windowe treatments and of Antique Floors,
Of pictures of the Great and sometimes Good,
Of Sideboards, Cutlery and Foreign Food.
They then depart in fullsome spending humours,
Wielding their credit cards like true Consumers.

The Open House is partly for Prestige,
Also, in part, some say, Noblesse Oblige,
To build Repute, an elevated Perch,
And raise some Moneys for the local Church.
We hope they neither fret nor greatly care
About attendant candy-papers, wear and tear,
Or sticky fingers. And we dearly trust
They do not care about the dirt and dust.
We also hope they never overheard
Some comments from among ye Common Herde:

"That colour doesn't go in here at all,
And I'd remove the intervening wall."
"They've muddled modern stuff with the antiques."
"The Drapes don't match at all, that floorboard creaks."
"This Roome looks empty, that is far too fulle."
"The Pictures second-rate, both olde and dulle."
"This Shelfe has not been dusted for three Weekes."
"The bassin in the downstairs toilet leakes."
(Yet think of the time and efforte that it took
To reddy all so they could come and looke!)

It's Human Natur thus to picke apart
That which is done in genuine well-meant parte.
To cavil, carpe and playe the wise and knowing,
To dream imagined Splendours while you're crowing;
And boost yourself when you are thereby faced
With evidence of far superior Taste.
The Critics have for sure an unfair Edge—
The unexampled dubious Privilege—
Of never having to themselves endure
Their own visit from the Spring House Toure.

Wen ye next Aprylle turns its annual Course
Then house-bounde wimmin will again in force
Enjoy the birdyes and the freshe Springe aire
That in their Citye is so pure and clare.
They'll folde their Pullovers and winter Smockes,
And don their Sneakers and forego their Sockes.
With back-packes, visors and reluctant Spouses,
They will examine *different* Rich Men's Houses.
No owner wants to undergo, I'm sure
For two years running Georgetowne's Spring House Toure.

In Praise of Old Houses

There's nothing appealing in touching the ceiling
In a box on an eighth of an acre.
Nor would a garage, be it ever so large
Induce me to be its caretaker.
It isn't sufficient to be heat-efficient
Or to have super-power in your showers,
If the walls are so thin that your close neighbour's din
Keeps you wakeful and fretful for hours.

Nor do I like the McMansions
With kitchens the size of a block.
By the kilowatt-hour the power they devour
Would give General Motors a shock.
With a house that extensive, it gets, like, expensive
You'd feel that you lived on your own.
If you've news to impart, you are so far apart
That you talk to your wife on the phone.

These houses, now new, will get older,
As we who live in them grow old.
Their hasty erection will need fresh protection,
The hot water tank will grow cold.
Home theatres will be superseded,
The heating and drains need replacing.
Once the kids have left home and you're all on your own,
What an echoing barn you'll be facing.

I'll settle for age and high ceilings,
For a roof with occasional leaks,
For the visiting mouse in our historic house,
And for waiting for workmen for weeks.
The paintwork is chipped and needs fixing,
The wiring is ancient and frayed;
The floorboards are creaking, the plumbing needs tweaking,
But at least the mortgage is paid.

I call it an elegant splendour;
The proportions are human, just right.
The walls are in brick, reassuringly thick,
And you can't hear the neighbours at night.
As the planet gets hotter and hotter,
And the tempests and hurricanes blow,
He who espouses these flimsy new houses
Will be homeless, and where will he go?

Kefalonia

We came, we saw, we sunbathed

Odysseus, who came from an island next door,
Found Kefalonia a terrible bore.
No dragons, no beasties, no Charybdis or Scyllas,
Just a load of young Brits drinking beer in their villas.
From the earliest moment when he was a boy,
He wanted adventures, like leveling Troy.
But although he had traveled around quite a lot,
He seemed to ignore this particular spot.

Here people are friendly, the climate sublime,
The countryside scented with sage and with thyme.
The olives are ancient, the beaches are sandy,
The food is so-so, but the markets are handy.
But except for Corelli and his mandolin,
There is little to stimulate adrenaline.
It's an excellent place to just lie in the sun,
But nothing occurs here, when all's said and done.

No, history's passed by this particular isle—
A backwater now, as it's been for a while.
Top Romans arrived, found the island quite pleasant,
But generally gave it away as a present.
The Venetians came by and proved a mild menace,

But the wine wasn't good, so they went back to Venice.
The odd conqueror conquered, but promptly departed;
The British came too, but were rather half-hearted.

No sign of a palace of mythical kings,
No civilizations or mystical springs.
No rivers to hell and no acropoli
To attract foreign visitors happening by.
The hire cars are hired, but most sit in the sun,
For where would they go if they went for a run?
No wonder the Italians and British all choose
The beach and the poolside, banter and booze.

Choice

They think we'll rejoice,
Offered infinite choice.
But in fact more is less;
Indecision means stress.
Why think it is clever—
While wasting our time
(a maddening crime)—
To propose the adoption
Of every damned option
Under the sun,
Instead of just one?

Just take the car,
Where they've gone much too far.
Do I have to recap
The ten types of hubcap
The number of doors,
Colored carpets on floors,
The bumpers, the hoods,
Powered windows, faux-woods?
One mentally cowers
In the face of horsepowers,
Different colors and trims,
And personalized shims.

Take the cereals on offer:
A hundred they proffer,
And do so in aisles
Stretching out there for miles.
Vitamins added in endless array
In confusing proportions of C, D and A.
If you read all the labels,
Ingredient tables,
I very much fear
It would be a career.

Hi-tech sort of gear
Is a category where
They include lots of stuff
That you don't use enough,
Or remember it's there,
Or particularly care.
The shops you buy through
Mostly haven't a clue;
The instructions are vast,
And a whole day has passed
Before you work out
What the item's about.

Oh, take me back home
Where the buffaloes roam,
Where you rock in your chair
In fresh air with no care,
Where in the boondocks
The shops have small stocks,
And you're settled and done
With a "choice" of just one;
And you buy your provisions

With no endless decisions,
Just a simple invoice and
No multiple choice.

So who's going to tell
The people who sell
That we're doing just fine
Without overdesign?
Who's going to complain:
"Keep it simple and plain"?
Let it do just one task,
That's all that we ask.
I'll make a new start:
"Give us less à la carte!"
Come, you too can rejoice
With more time and less choice.

The Dinner Gift

Do you remember last time what we took?
A crime DVD or that Middle East book?
We've given them flowers and the odd potted plant,
And that recycled candle that came from your aunt.
And didn't we bring back some French *confiture*?
Perhaps that would do? Or the blackberry liqueur?
But hang on a moment, temper my zeal;
They brought that last time they came for a meal.

A cheese, I am certain, would go down quite well.
Unless they're intent on a low LDL.
A box of good chocolates is fine to donate,
Except that I know they are watching their weight.
What can we take without causing disquiet
For people who live on a permanent diet?
Oh, for a gift that is not anodyne!
We'll just have to take them a bottle of wine.

A Father Plays with His Son

No, Henry!
That's the clutch, it's not the gear.
Look at the plan, it goes down here,
In front of the driver in his cab.
It allows him to operate the grab.
The boom works now from left to right,
But stops near the ground; the nut's too tight.
Or maybe it needs a drop of oil.
Ah! Now it can scoop a load of soil.
I've still to add the left-hand track,
Adjust the tension, slightly slack.
Soon it will scoot across the floor.
Oh, where is that grub screw? What a bore!

Where's Henry? Oh well, he'll return.
Watching Dad is how kids learn.

Make sure the tracking is aligned,
And fix the license plate behind.
Well, here goes! Zap! Why, not a sound!
Come, get the batteries right way round!
Control it gently, mustn't jerk,
It's great to see that drive-train work.
Over the carpet to the door,
Pick up some Lego, now some more.

Isn't this fun? Now back again.
Avoiding the dumper and the crane . . .

"Daddy! Please come up and say goodnight
And bring a drink, if that's alright?"

Oh, Henry, yes, I'll be right there.
I've just one minor, last repair.

Light and Fit

The exercise culture is changing.
Diversity now is in fashion.
Those hoping to trim now go to the gym
They're lifting and stretching with passion.
"You have to do something aerobic,"
Says the trainer, now much in demand,
"Set the walking machine to twelve or thirteen,
And step out when I give the command."

The cross-trainer's used without ceasing,
The bicycles constantly whirr;
Young men with weights lift them hoping for dates,
And tills ring as gym owners purr.
Despite the obligatory music,
And the young girls who endlessly talk,
The fat and the frail, whether female or male,
Are trying to shed pounds as they walk.

But some of a larger dimension
Can train for all they are worth.
It's the size of portion that's out of proportion
And accounts for expansion of girth.
Let them strengthen the pectoral muscles,
Make certain their posture is good.
But for them to live longer and lighter and stronger,
Let them eat a little less food.

Recital Time

Recital time at the keyboard.
We've been going through this for years.
No "Plunking it out for Beginners"
Or songs about gondoliers.
No, this is for serious students,
Some destined for Juilliard.
They play fugues and preludes,
And Chopin *Études*,
But whatever they play, it is hard.

They all have in common a teacher,
Who's devoted himself to his art.
The succession of tutors before him
Reaches back, so they say, to Mozart.
He can tinkle a riff from Duke Ellington,
Or a dissonant offering from Pärt.
Perhaps you have heard
His Rachmaninoff Third
Which he's recently mastered by heart?

So this is his Great Exhibition,
His students are strutting their stuff.
Their families are numbed by their practice,
But have they practiced enough?
Each enters the hall a bit nervous.
The Steinway stands there, looking black.

Some young lad is cursed,
For he has to go first,
While the others look glum at the back.
So here is the next little maestro.
Good heavens! She looks about nine.
Composed as a junior ice-maiden,
She plays like a young Rubinstein.
The third is not a lot older;
He has his Beethoven down pat.
His diminuendo
That came at the end, oh!
I'd have listened all morning to that!

Some players played without music.
Oh, for a young and clear brain!
No losing your place at bar thirty
And starting all over again.
Do you think they have time to watch videos?
Or for hanging out with their pals?
Will they, measure for measure,
Work hard with such pleasure,
When it's time to start dating the gals?

And last, perhaps least, comes her moment.
My wife is alone on the stage.
She plays Bach, marked as "molto allegro,"
Which is fearfully hard at our age.
What comes out is a stately "andante."
Dexterity's not at its peak!
What a youngster can do in a minute or two
Takes us seniors more like a week.

This is the truth about music:
It contravenes natural law,
In which competence grows with experience,
And knowledge and age overawe.
But not in the business of music!
Here, the younger and nimbler the fingers
The more do their owners excel,
Leaving us to complain, stumbling through it again,
"Last week I was playing it well."

So here is the moral I'm preaching:
Starting at fifty's too late.
Maybe those on guitar
Can start slow and get far,
But piano? You need to be eight.

The Sun Umbrella

I sat on the rooftop that Tuesday in June.
A strong wind was blowing, a warm afternoon.
The umbrella above, as shade from the sun,
Was anchored (I thought) and could not be undone.

Four floors beneath me, some yards from my feet,
The traffic moved down the arterial street.
On my open-top aerie I sat and reflected
That the bustle below could scarce be suspected.

When all of a sudden, and to my disgust,
Came out of the blue an extraordinary gust.
Seizing the brollie this violent updraft
Made it spin in the air like an alien craft.

Then over the capstone in less than a beat
The brollie and pole disappeared to the street.

Did I panic? Well, yes! And I seriously thought
What a claimant might say in a magistrate's court.

(He:)
"This missile, your honour, came sudden, unseen,
Like a bolt from the blue; it was striped white and green.
This wasn't, it seemed, an incompetent error,
But a fiendish new strike in the great war on terror."

(Or, she:)
"I was on my way home with my son, who's aged seven,
When a bright green umbrella descended from heaven,
And just like a rocket clear out of the sun,
It damaged my cellphone and skewered my son."

I just didn't believe it! Disaster! Not that!
And I leapt down the stairs like a young scalded cat.
No sirens were blaring, no signs of a crowd,
No ambulance men, no police, and no shroud.

But trace of the parasol I couldn't see.
Was it high above London or caught in a tree?
And then I looked down and there I beholded
My green striped umbrella intact, neatly folded.

I crossed the street quickly, a leap and a bound,
And breathed once again; now it lay on the ground.
I said to it, "Thank you! Did you give me a fright!
You're o.k.? You're undamaged? You had a good flight?"

The Allotment

Allotments in the First World War were planned
To grow fresh produce on some public land.
For a small outlay you then could fashion
A veggie plot to add to meager ration.
Still now men linger in a chair and doze
While some huge marrow effortlessly grows.
They dream of taking this fine merchandise
To competitions, where they'll win first prize.

Ah, things to eat! Now that has huge appeal!
Fresh vegetables to supplement a meal.
Just soil and seed and rain, a hoe, and sun,
And soon a hundredweight, or half a ton
Of carrot, lettuce, broad bean, beet and pea
Appear by Nature's magic—and all free!
The atavistic pleasure and the gain
Of being just a peasant once again!

So, for the last some hundred years of toil
Have men kept healthy, digging up the soil.
They are but farmers in a gent's disguise,
Who, lacking cows and sheep, must compromise;
But have the joy of telling guests, "Mmh, pardon,
This broccoli I grew in my own garden.
The apples in the apple pie—a must—
Came from my plot, without, of course, the crust".

My younger son acquired such new allotment
(Lack of experience clearly lent enchantment).
Describing it to father on the phone,
He told me it was rather over-grown.
But if I'd like to do some gentle weeding
Why, soon on new potatoes we'd be feeding.
Tomatoes, beans and sweetcorn would be sown
And many other goodies would be grown.

I came. I saw. I failed to conquer.

There, before us, luxuriant, to be weeded
Were all the invasive species ever seeded—
Bindweed, stinkweed, fireweed, mayweed, juneweed,
Pokeweed, ragweed, hogweed, knapweed, allweed—
Every rank creeper, twining vine, and wort
Had, with brute force and muscle to be fought.
Every thistle, bramble, grass and clover,
Known to man gave ground its verdant cover.

Then came the spade and digging; oh, the shock!
The surface soil resembled solid rock.
Backs start to ache, the tough spade creaks
In iron-hard earth un-rained upon for weeks.
Water helps to counteract the bake,
But this tough ground required a huge, great lake.
And once you broke the surface, the dismay!
For underneath the earth was sticky clay.

Nearby, well fed, some fattened magpies lurked,
And watched us, smirking, chattering, while we worked,
Hoping to steal some blackberries, undetected.
We scurried around to get the fruit protected.

The radishes next to the berries put
Were accidentally trampled underfoot.
Which was a shame, for since their early sowing
They were the only vegetables growing.

William is young and strong and might just see
(When he has reached the age of sixty-three)
His garden tamed and in productive glory
(Although I won't be there to hear the story).
By then he'll hope to have all wild weeds banned—
Alas, they'll still sneak back to claim the land.
Although of gardening I'm a stout proponent,
Clearly, Nature is a tough opponent.

Meanwhile, it's probably unwise to stop
Buying leeks and onions at the shop.

PERSONAL TO ME

Me

Ah, those fleeting first memories of when I was young—
And three;
Then the pain of those nasty bullies at school—
So I flee;
And the master who gives me a passage in French—
A précis;
The holiday journeys to Scotland and France—
Carefree;

And the sailing on "Carmen" with father in charge—
Burgee;*
Those years in the barracks, the uniform, drill—
Draftee;
The thrill when awarded just better than "B"—
Good degree;
The first proper girlfriend I take to a dance—
Whoopee!

The very first job when I haven't a clue—
Employee;
I've found my first wife and the wedding takes place—
Marquee;
Those stories of how I just flew down the slopes—
Après-ski;
I'm at home on the stage where I wish I could stay—
Emcee;

I've bought a new house that I cannot afford—
Mortgagee;
There are long export trips to the ends of the earth—
Gum tree;
And to places exotic on a wing and a prayer—
Rupee;
I'm managing people who don't fall in line—
Ennui!

And I privately send both my children to school—
High fee;
With intolerable worry and stress I panic—
And flee;
Now I've worked thirty years and I'm done—
Oh, the glee!
All those turbulent years at the firm—
Now I'm free!

Now I've time for creation, reflection and friends—
More tea?
I meet a new wife living over the sea—
In D.C.
The travels in Tuscany, Pompeii, and Rome—
Napoli.
Great musicals written, seen only by me—
Do-re-mi!

The luncheons and chatter at Café Milano—
Devotee;
The dinners with people as smart as can be—
Repartee.
But now I am creaky and grumpy and old—
Bad knee;

But the pension from work has been tied to inflation—
Yippee!

Of a sudden a new generation appears—
Bootee;
And they're cute as can be and exactly like me—
Pedigree;
Now a grandfather's something that happens to others—
Not me!
And one day it's likely to happen to you—
You'll see!

I've a new lease on life, and it's great and it's good!—
Yessiree!
It's just as fantastic as being a Dad—
Guarantee!
I've everything possible a man can require—
And foresee;
Can I take my dear wife on departure—
Suttee?

*Burgee: a small masthead flag, a wind direction indicator

Aphrodite

Said Apollo the God
To the belle Aphrodite,
"Come hither, my lovely
And take off your nightie."

"Oh no, Sir," said she
(the advice of her mother),
"You're a hunk, this I know,
But I'm seeking another.

"He'll be tall, he'll be fair
And more handsome than you,
Who sits on this mountain with
Nothing to do.

"He'll draw hippos all day
And compose on the lyre,
With a figure to die for
And kisses like fire.

"But it's eons B.C. and I've
Yet to discover
A single male person
Resembling this lover."

So the sweet Aphrodite
Set out on her quest,
But no human or god
Passed her rigorous test.

She travelled through Tartary,
Turkey and Spain,
Togo, Jamaica—
The men were all vain.

She went to Peru,
But the men were untrue,
And a diet of buffalo
Ruled out the Sioux.

Women were servants to
Indians and Medes,
And the muscular Swedes
Couldn't cope with her needs.

There was nothing much going in
Vietnam or Gaul.
In Nepal, so it's said,
She found no one at all.

In Italy she had
No great expectations.
Though, be fair, Italians are the
Best dressed of nations.

In the Marches of Italy,
Well, *quel surprise!*

On a soggy, wet day with
Mud up to her knees,

And after a search for
Thousands of years
She found what she looked for
In joy and in tears.

A visit to England
Was first soundly rejected!
Good gracious, she thought,
This is quite unexpected.

She thought Brits were boring,
Standoffish, and plain,
That the country was shrouded
In fog and in rain.

Well . . . .
He drew hippos all day and
Composed on the lyre,
With a figure to die for and
Kisses like fire.

He told endless stories and
Laughed far too much,
But she curiously responded to
Laughter and touch.

And now for all goddesses
It has been written:
"If you're wise you'll discover
Your lovers in Britain."

A Cigar on the Porch

*In praise of cigars, and how I was once fool enough
to smoke them.*

A cigar on the porch I admit is a sin,
And indicates squarely the age-group I'm in.
"Poor fellow," they tell me, "You must understand,
Your pleasures in life are now frowned on or banned.
Sugar is fattening, ice cream forbidden—
If you think about sex then keep it well hidden!
Driving? Not on, your reactions are slow,
And your bones are too brittle to walk in the snow."

Ah! Cigars on the porch! Any ten "Senoritas"
Beat ten margaritas or ten Bach partitas.
With a cocktail I sip and my sorrows I drown,
But I end rather maudlin, as the level goes down.
With Bach's music the harmony, cadence and tune
Are balm to the soul, but they're over too soon.
While cigars on the porch and a view of the flowers
Are peaceful diversions that go on for hours.

A puff on the porch is an aid to reflection
A small interlude for some self-introspection.
How to stay slim and avoid gaining weight?
The faux pas at parties I'm prone to of late . . .

The dozens of emails composed with such care,
Unanswered, they're lost in the ether. But where?
There's no answer, in fact, no point in the Why?
Just light up another and gaze at the sky.

With one's pungent aromas one slips from the house,
A mark of respect for a tolerant spouse.
A solitary moment, no risk of disruption,
The fumes guarantee against chance interruption.
But the downside is climate; the temperature veers
Rapidly down when the wintertime nears.
So I do all my thinking 'twixt May and September—
A cigar on the porch ain't much fun in December.

Maturity

Now I'm mature I can sense in my heart
That it happened too late and I'm falling apart.
It's not just attention I'm tending to lack,
But my abs are less tight and my biceps are slack.
My hair, once a forest, now looks like a moor,
I was once eagle-eyed, but my eyesight's now poor.
My hearing's all right on the second repeat,
I'd rather not mention the state of my feet.
I was only just telling a friend, by the way . . .
Damn!
I've totally lost what I wanted to say.

Breakfast Alone

Breakfast alone. Ah, yes, breakfast alone!
An essential in every insomniac's home.
You'll be hearing the sufferer firmly intone,
"I need breakfast alone, give me breakfast alone!"

So I get up at six and I stumble around,
Cursing under my breath till the dressing gown's found.
I creep down the stairs in the Stygian gloom,
For in winter it's dark, pitch-black as a tomb.

Breakfast alone. Ah, yes, breakfast alone!
I need time to wake up without chatter or phone.
A police siren's wail can elicit a groan.
I need breakfast alone. Ah, yes, breakfast alone!

Automaton-like then I boil me an egg,
And I stagger around on my arthritic leg.
I make huge pots of tea, then with butter and bread,
I creep back upstairs and collapse into bed.

You'll have noticed I'm sure that a dog with a bone
Will ignore those around him and gnaw it alone.
He will jealously guard it, not wanting to chat,
And will even ignore the approach of a cat.

And equally sacred is breakfast to me.
The cure for my sleeplessness surely is tea.
For the tired and confused it is also the key;
Just be patient! I'll come to! Soon I'll be me!

Breakfast alone. Ah, yes, breakfast alone!
I need peace while the house is as still as a stone.
All I hear from my wife's an occasional groan,
Which suits me just fine—I need breakfast alone.

And slowly but surely the blood in my veins
Is pumped to my feet and my hands and my brains.
Despite grumpy replies that are barely benign,
I'll be perfectly civil and nice around nine.

Breakfast alone. Ah, yes, breakfast alone!
The importance of silence is largely unknown.
If you do have to speak, please, a soft monotone.
Breakfast alone. Ah, yes, breakfast alone!

Swimming

On my deckchair I sit in thrall,
Watching Martha do the crawl.
How had they so easily taught her
To swim so fast, head under water?
How does she flash through ocean swell,
Waggle her legs and breathe as well,
While I'm the sort of land-locked bloke
Who much prefers the breast, er, stroke.

Hotel Beds

Hotel ads the world around
With clever marketing abound.
Their rates, they claim, are total steals,
With rebates and with weekend deals,

With stunning views from every room,
Facilities for bride and groom,
The beaches manicured and clean,
The top suites fit for king and queen.

The thick piled carpet, dim-lit bars,
The restaurant boasting Michelin stars,
The gym, the sauna and the spa
Outshine competitors by far.

All this is fine, though hardly cheap.
But truthfully I'm there to sleep.
Oh what a joy if they instead
Concentrated on the BED!

This furnishing that so enrages
Hasn't changed since Middle Ages.
Flat, resistant, unforgiving
It's more for torture than for living.

A third of *your* life and my own
Is spent, not in a bar, but prone,

Engaged in sleep or peccadillo
Between two sheets, with head on pillow.

I am a born insomniac
Who cannot sleep on side or back.
I toss around. Oh, what a way
To spend my annual holiday!

Hoteliers must as a breed
Get easily the sleep they need,
Not for them the guest who wheedles:
"All night I've had the pins and needles."

They must think the room is cheap.
Who cares if occupants don't sleep?
And this explains their inattention,
Lack of care, incomprehension.

Complaints, in some hoteliers' eyes,
Come truly as a great surprise.
"We offer luxury in this hotel.
We have to help them sleep as well?"

Why can't all hotels compete
By offering us *all* a treat?
For those who like beds hard as brick
Let them to their preference stick.

But let the rest whose skin is thin
Get softer beds when they check in.
Me? I can't take it anymore;
I may as well sleep on the floor!

My Prostate

Unless the family lore is lying,
By this age I should be dying.
My forebear males in days of yore
Got cancer at about three score,
But didn't know it till too late
And passed away 'round sixty-eight,
The victims of some errant gene,
Unsuspected and unseen.
The prostate felt the first attack,
Then cancer spread to front and back.

The doctors then ascribed the cause
To old age and to Nature's laws;
At sixty I was shocked to learn
I had the problem in my turn.
The time was ripe, the gene switched on,
And there was I damn nearly gone,
Confirmed with signs of threatening tumour
That taxed my faltering sense of humour.
I made my Will, I said goodbye.
I then prepared myself to die.

Then, lo! appeared a surgeon who
Knew precisely what to do.
Equipped with scalpel and with mask,
And more than equal to the task:

Doctor Regan, hero, man of vision,
The master of precise incision,
Who's battled all the worst prostates
Throughout these great United States;
Who quietly heals, pray let me note,
While others boast and self-promote.

A skillful surgeon, credit he
To Georgetown University.
"Fear not," said he, "I'll see you through.
I guarantee you good as new."
He cut, I slept, and he, adept,
His promises he more than kept.
I woke, I hurt, the feeling passed,
And I was on my feet at last.

Five years have gone, you'd never guess
That I was ever in that mess.
I'm hale and fit and full of life.
Don't take my word, just ask my wife.

Kensington Church, 1944

A true story: the bombing of this church is my first vivid memory. The name of the organist was never recorded.

It is March and the firebombs fall out of the sky
From the Luftwaffe bombers that chance to pass by.
The ack-ack guns fire and the searchlights all search,
But a bomb hits the nave of Kensington Church.

The roof catches fire like some tinder in drought,
And Londoners gather amid the blackout.
Around them the flames and the billowing smoke
Swirl up the street as the bystanders choke.

The din of the sirens, the call of "All Clear"
As fire engines, flashing, come here and go there.
First-aiders and nurses, St. John's, the Home Guard
Form a long water-chain through the streets and churchyard.

The roof is ablaze and flames lick the clouds,
An unspoken fear is gripping the crowds:
Will the steeple burn too and collapse in the fire,
Destroying the altar, the vestry, the choir?

Like huge throbbing snakes the fire hoses curl round,
As the fire engines pump to a crackling sound.

Hauled high up the ladders, the hoses astream
Keep dousing the inferno midst huge clouds of steam.

Then the vicar arrives, looks alarmed at the sight,
And he thanks those nearby for their resolute fight.
His concern is the organ, "A fine one, it's said.
It's the water, not smoke, that I specially dread.

"It's standard; that keyboard, a typical type.
The problem's if water gets into a pipe.
It's bound to be ruined, of that there's no doubt,
But if played at full volume the water blows out."

At this the organist shouts, "Wait a bit.
I'm going in there and I'm rescuing it!"
"No, no," cries the vicar, "that's too great a risk."
His protest is powerful, his manner is brisk.

"It's my duty, don't worry," the organist cries;
And the fumes and the heat he bravely defies.
He struggles through debris, avoiding the flame,
And wishes to leave just as fast as he came.

But he starts up the organ and plays to the beat,
And the music he plays can be heard in the street.
And the water that rains down to put out the fire
Is expelled up the organ pipes into the choir.

His repertoire varies from waltzes to swing
But most of the time he plays "God Save the King."
And thus to the enemy gives a riposte
Braving smoke, fire, and water at personal cost.

With a crash, a spark-shower, and great waves of heat,
The roof of the nave falls ablaze at his feet.
Then the bell-ringers join in, a round starts to ring,
And along with the bells he plays "God Save the King."

I am five, and my grandmother runs from the flat,
In her sensible shoes and her pre-World War hat.
She sprints down the street to the clanging alarms,
And she carries me safe in her sheltering arms.

Oh, the thrill: all the firemen, the uniforms, noise,
The engines and smoke that delight little boys!
The water describing an arc in the air,
The thrill as the tongues of the blazing roof flare!

"You shouldn't take risks with those bombers around,
With a kiddie like that you should be underground."
"I don't reckon with shelters," says Gran, "never fret,
I've survived for four years and they've not got me yet."

But her words are drowned out by a creak and a crack
As the roof of the nave falls in flames at the back
To the shouts of dismay from the onlooking crowds,
While the steeple untouched stands proud in the clouds.

Sparks and black smoke fill the darkening sky,
And some ash in the air makes this little boy cry.
But the pain is forgotten—the bells start to ring.
Unheard in the background is "God Save the King."

Dancing at the Ritz

In ballroom (not in rock-and-roll)
You are a man in full control.
You spin, you whirl, you slide, you glide,
Leaving your partner mystified.
With no option but to hope
Your muscled arms will calmly cope,
You wonder what you'd have in store
Were she to tumble on the floor.

To avoid us ending on our backs
I whisper to her, "Just relax."
This otherwise might cause a riot,
But now she's looking calm and quiet.
Some say the steps should be exact;
To me the dancing is an act,
A chance to show my style close-up.
As for the steps, I make them up.

Those ladies dining at the Ritz
Used to its glamourous, gilded glitz,
Observing our creative waltz
Wouldn't know genuine from false.
If you are smooth, your back is straight,
You're in command, you dominate.
You confidently smile, and more—
You don't hit others on the floor,

Women give an envious glance,
And sigh, "Can those two dance!"
After a perfunctory kerfuffle
They join the dance and grimly shuffle.
We, on the other hand, enjoy it.
We dress up once a year, Savoy it,
To feel one up on, who can tell?
Men who could buy the whole hotel?

Who are the fools? Guys overeating?
Or us on the dance-floor, overheating?
They with their paunches and diseases?
Or me with hips and creaky kneeses?
They smoke cigars, sip one last tipple,
While I? Will I end up a cripple?
And homebound, upon a London bus,
I ask, "Who's smart, those guys or us?"

A CONTRARIAN'S VIEW

I Did It All Myself

An entrepreneur speaks out . . .

I did it all myself.
For sure, I did it all myself.
I never used networks or old college friends
On whom the success of so many depends.
I went out to work at the age of eighteen
Thin as a rake, but determined and lean,
And I laid rows of bricks and mixed tons of cement,
Made ten bucks a day for my food and my rent.

Twelve hours with no break did I labor on site,
And I did my book-learning by candle at night.
Then one day the boss man said, "Hey, come here, kid,
I've been watching you, boy, and I like what you did.
You've got brains, you work hard, but your problem is knowledge."
So I took myself off to community college.
I learned my house-building from sewer to gable,
And earned extra money by waiting on table.

Then I built up a company, just as I'd planned,
Scouring the country, developing land.
I have been real successful, the business has grown,
And I've ten million bucks that I've made on my own.
I'd have made twice as much and could maybe relax
If it weren't for government, liberals, and tax,

The planners, the lawyers, the dumb regulations,
Activist judges, red-tape strangulations;

And NIMBYs who get up a great caterwaul
When you build on a green field a new shopping mall.
It's always the do-gooding, meddling few
Who complain at the loss of some trees or a view.
No, all the restrictions should now be relaxed
And government prohibitions be axed.
We don't need these laws, they all need upending,
And let's call a halt to all government spending.

Send bureaucrats off up to Mars in a rocket.
Stop pilfering profit from my hard-earned pocket.
Sack all pen-pushers, ignore stupid rules
Made for the work-shy and drawn up by fools.
No, I've never had handouts or government aid;
I worked hard, but fairly—for that I was paid.
This fuss about poverty's all overblown.
After all, what I've done, I have done on my own.

. . . Truth replies

Are you telling me your parents had nothing to do
With the bundle of talents and hangups that's you?
Where is the mention of school on your part,
That taught you the culture and gave you a start?
You must owe a debt to some of your teachers,
Those lousily paid and unrecognized creatures.
Who established the college you studied at later?
It wasn't the wages you earned as a waiter.

Who paid for the roads that we all take for granted?
Our whole infrastructure was not simply planted,

But grew from decades of investment, and sacks
Of public subventions you now spurn as "tax."
Who bought your houses, your suburban sprawls,
Your gas stations, offices, car parks and malls?
Why, government workers, contractors and such,
And similar folk whom you now hate so much.

The Fortune Five Hundred fattens and waxes
On recycled money from federal taxes;
Directly or not, here's a thought to astound:
You probably shared in this merry-go-round!
Who laid the ground rules that draw to this nation
Immigrants swelling a huge population,
All needing housing? These guys you can thank
For increasing your profits and cash in your bank.

What is the value you put upon peace,
Containment of crime and the role of police?
Have you had no advantage from new medication?
Nearly half the research is paid from taxation.
Have you not been protected from rules governing drugs,
Or water we drink, free of threatening bugs?
I bet, were you sick, I would hear through your sobs
"Wish they'd get a grip and start doing their jobs."

Scrap Social Security? Wow, you are plucky,
But perhaps, just like you, everyone will get lucky—
The market might rise and its rise might not vary,
Believe that? Believe in the good Christmas Fairy!
Thank God for the people who faithfully strive
To frame equal rules which let businesses thrive,
Where corruption is modest, the playing field fair,
And the whole business culture's not governed by fear.

You'd have a real reason to grumble and moan
If you had to do business in Sierra Leone.
No, none of us prosper alone, I would say.
A little humility goes a long way.

The Bonobos

Life comes, life goes, and not much changes.
The pecking order rearranges.
Perhaps one day the human race
Will quit this Earth and in its place,
In half a million years or so,
We'll have the ruling bonobo.

This happy ape is now well-known
For almost no testosterone.
Eschewing violence and force,
It solves disputes by intercourse,
Explaining why you can't efface
The knowing smile upon its face.

Bonobos seldom prowl the trees
Fighting over territories,
Or seek aggression therapy
Swinging through the canopy.
But like the gentle turtledove
They coo, and end up making love.

A Fantasy

Bonobos watched with canny sense
The foolish homo sapiens
With gay abandon multiply,

Polluting earth and sea and sky
And casually wondering why
He choked to death as time went by.

And thus he died, alas, unmourned,
Still deaf to warnings he had scorned.
In centuries the Earth recovered.
In time the bonobos discovered
The vacuum left by Man's demise,
And started to extemporize.

Down from the trees in which they dwelt,
They stood upright to scour the veldt.
Their speech developed from a grunt,
They sallied forth with clubs to hunt.
And (this the current bonobo loathes)
They soon got used to wearing clothes.

Then came the fire and then the wheel.
Soon came spears and iron and steel.
Then they dreamt up government
In forms they hadn't really meant.
Developers emerged as from the murk,
Made loads of dosh without much work.

And facile ones became adroit
At how to bargain and exploit.
Relationships, once amatory
Began to be perfunctory.
Life became all slap and dash,
And rush and stress and making cash.

Of course by now had come the priest,
Who promised heaven when deceased,

Provided they refused to pet
And cuddle everyone they met.
"This undermines our family life.
Do it in private, with your wife."

Not knowing who your father was
Can have some benefits because
It makes the group the family,
Reducing petty rivalry.
This once-relaxed society
Became consumed with jealousy.

Fights broke out between the males
And gossip ruled, and tattletales.
And as the population grew
Great wars occurred as if on cue.
Competition (never done)
Now spread to almost everyone.

The rich got rich, the poor got poor
Some weak apes starved and furthermore
Where once there had been space for all
Great cities grew and with them sprawl.
The air got foul, the water rank;
The ghettoes and the barrios stank.

Now there were no knowing smiles,
No forest lush for miles and miles,
No sensitivity, no love,
Just acid rain from up above.
And as the centuries went by
Most wondered what they'd lost, and why.

The Neo (ha!) Liberals

It comes at a price, this so-called reform
That took both the US and Britain by storm.
When Marx was a threat they looked over their shoulders
And had to throw bones to the common householders,
Offering benefits—dole, pensions, health,
And tax on the rich to redistribute wealth.
But the Soviets gone and the Left in decline,
The neo (ha!) liberals can be less benign.

It started with High Priests who came from Chicago,
Determined to place a lasting embargo
On national health schemes and help for the poor,
On social security, dole pay and more.
Privatization became the new fashion,
Prescribed for the world with a dogmatic passion.
This brand of religion's a thing to behold!
Those treasures we paid for are now bought and sold.

"So much more efficient, so much less a drain,
Things work so much better for corporate gain.
Just look at Italians! Just look at the French!
Their rates of employment make capitalists blench!
The unions, bureaucracy, benefits, rules,
Show them to be, economically, fools!"
Caring for sick people and helping the poor
Are cruelly dismissed by the rich who want more.

So where do we go in this new paradigm?
One possible outcome's an increase in crime.
If there's no safety net and no hope, well you feel it,
If you now can't earn it, maybe you can steal it.
I'd argue poor funding for state education
Is the start of decline for a prosperous nation.
Work pressure is greater, the hours of work longer,
The loyalty's gone, your self-interest's stronger.

The conventionally sick can still find a cure,
But God help the patient whose ills are obscure!
God help the middle-aged thrown out of work!
God help the indigent, crazy, berserk!
Pity the mother alone with four kids,
And the pensionless women and men on the skids.
God help the institutionalized old;
If you don't have the cash then you're out in the cold.

We used to believe we should all share and care,
But gradually we see what's happening here
(Unprotested by media who cannot be trusted),
The old Social Contract is terminally busted.
And creeping upon us the ultimate bungle:
A return to the biblical law of the jungle!

Climate Change—An Apology

What will they say of us when we are gone,
When it dawns on them all that we very well knew
(As they wrestle with flooding, starvation and storms)
Of the turmoil their world would be struggling through?

What will they think of us (selfishly set
Upon motors and holidays, easily bought)
And the choking pollution discharged in the air
We contribute to blithely with scarcely a thought?

Will they wonder at pineapples flown from Hawaii
While the frost and the snow are still thick on the ground?
Fresh flowers from Colombia, well out of season,
At a cost to the planet, unseen but profound?

Will they say: "Our grandparents, whom we still remember,
Knew that the pole-ice was melting away.
They heard the debates about currents and oceans,
But greeted each fact with a passive dismay.

"They knew in their hearts that some real sacrifice
Was required, some remedial money and labour.
They said the right things, but still hoped against hope
That appropriate restraint would commence with their neighbour.

"They worried a lot about hurricanes, storms,
And the lot of the seals and the few polar bears.
But they sighed with relief when the skeptics said 'Whoa,
It won't happen (at least, not for fifty-odd years).'

"'Don't worry,' they said, 'keep the growth rolling on.
Keep spending and wasting, don't take the full brunt
The grandkids will have to shape up or ship out;
For if it's an issue it's tough to confront.

"'We agree there's a problem. Solutions are hard.
The science is sound and now fully attested.
But big money talks, we're needing the income.
And the interests? Well, you can guess, they are vested.'"

Our grandchildren will say, "So the power plants belched on.
And at some point the balance just toppled and tipped,
Mother Nature triumphant is taking Her toll,
And our wings and our lives are thwarted and clipped.

"Now the sea levels rise and the lowlands are swamped.
There are millions of homeless of every race.
And nations once stable are riven with warfare
And death stalks the Earth at a gathering pace.

"Fresh water's a problem, high prices of food,
And flooding at unusual times of the year.
With business disrupted and jobs on the line,
People are nervous, distracted with fear.

"Southern Europe's becoming a desert with sand;
Its desperate people are trekking up north

Joined by North Africans, starving and sick,
Who'll be turned back or halted at gunpoint henceforth.

"Yes, we curse the short-sighted, the venal, the blind,
Who carelessly caused us this terrible plight,
Who lived comfortable lives in a state of denial
And whose gifts to the world were, in retrospect, slight.

"Some who were bought created bogus statistics;
They twisted the science, unconscionably lied.
Some bullied the serious people who warned them.
And none had the courage and faith to decide."

Man will react, if at all, in a crisis,
When the ambitious and greedy have backs to the wall.
Now speeches and meetings are all we can offer.
I apologize, kids, for us all to you all.

John Kenneth Galbraith

John Kenneth Galbraith, John Kenneth Galbraith
A "mischievous man"* in whose views we have faith,
Who *kicks at the pricks* and who strikes the right chord
And who tells us the "market" is "innocent fraud";
Who points out investor control is a sham,
And that those with the power don't give a god-damn,
As long as the salary merry-go-round
Rewards them with figures that simply astound.

"X is paid zillions, we have to compete."
"The global economy" is the conceit.
So, ever upward, increase the hordes
Of CEOs steering their compliant boards.
For those who enjoy these monetary lures
Have seldom, in fact, been true entrepreneurs.
They look handsome, say "yes," and are good diplomats,
And have stabbed in the back like true bureaucrats.

They play the right cards, their manner is brisk,
But not once in their lives have they taken a risk.
They're never accountable, seldom pay tax,
And you cannot get at them by phone or by fax.
Why do we tolerate thinking short-term,
When it undermines both workers and firm?
Why do we leave all these CEOs free,
To leave trails of destruction at each company?

And what, if it comes to that, sets them apart
From government workers who try and are smart,
Who look handsome, say "yes," and are good diplomats,
And who stab in the back like true bureaucrats?
Damn all (as per Galbraith). So why have they made
A hundred times more than the pen-pusher's paid?

*Quote from Howard Davies's *Guardian* review of *The Economics
of Innocent Fraud* by John Kenneth Galbraith, 7th August 2004

What Is the Point?

A bunch of bold earthlings set off for the stars,
Leaving behind them their mansions and cars.
Past comets and meteors, they traveled through space,
To spread the Good News of the great human race.

Economists, millionaires, social Darwinians,
Press commentators with right-wing opinions,
Missionary Baptists, all totally Right,
And a thousand Marines in case of a fight.

Their object? Imparting to all of creation
The superior values they hold as a nation:
Democracy, liberty, freedom, and truth
For galaxies distant and aliens uncouth.

They visited moons and heavenly spheres,
But most of these venues had thin atmospheres.
When one day they arrived at a planet with girth
And air, seas, and mountains exactly like Earth.

The water was clean and the air it was pure,
And the scenery looked like a tourist brochure.
No gas stations, concrete, no jerry-built mall,
No black-belching trucks, and no ads and no sprawl.

The beaches were pristine and in every stream
Were non-farmed young salmon and unpoisoned bream.

The missionary Leader, with broad Texan drawl,
Said "This seems like an opportune visit, ya'll."

*

But imagine his shock when the spacecraft descended!
His sense of the proper was deeply offended.
The people seemed happy! So what had gone wrong?
They laughed and they joked and they burst into song.

Their children were disciplined, slim and polite,
And the cats didn't yowl and the dogs didn't bite.
No President present to lay down the law,
No priests to be found there to justify war.

No lawyers or lobbyists, or millionaires
To leave their huge fortunes to vacuous heirs.
No poor forced to live on a minimum wage,
Or elders to grub out an anxious old age.

No, the people had leisure, worked two hours a day,
Unconcerned as they were about bosses and pay.
The community cared for them all from their birth
(Which couldn't be said for the people from Earth).

"This is all very well," said the economists,
"But we think there is something these people have missed.
Productivity's low. If they worked for more hours
Their economy could be successful, like ours."

The Social Darwinians said, "God has forgot
To decide who's successful and, alas, who is not.

In His absence we feel it's our job to ensure
That some people are rich and that others are poor."

"None of the people have been born again,"
Said the ministers, "witness their pain.
We'll have to persuade them the Rapture is nigh,
When half will be saved and the other half die."

The thousand bold soldiers were shocked to the corps.
"How can they live without slaughter and war?
This pacifist Heaven must now be destroyed.
If it caught on on Earth, we'd be unemployed."

So all those who bowed to the tough moneylenders,
Who were selfish and greedy, with various agendas,
Plus columnists offering bogus advice,
Set out to destroy this true Paradise.

And then came a strange and a wondrous event!
The natives immediately saw their intent:
"You can pull the wool over the eyes of Latinos
Or dumb Europeans or poor Filipinos.

But we stand for life full of fun, food, and laughter.
Your money's no use in the life ever after."
We have studied their meaning, and now it's agreed
They accused the invaders of unfathomable greed!

What is the point?

"What is the point of your ten-hour work days,
With two weeks, if that, as your paid holidays?
What possible gain would our people accrue
From dismantling the safety net to benefit you?

"Why should we earn a declining real wage,
And be dumped just as soon as we reach middle age?
Why should we tolerate people with wealth
And see a decline in our medical health?

What is the point?

"We don't need your priests and we don't need your nuns,
We hate violent movies and don't need your guns.
We don't need your drugs, your police, Coca-Cola,
Your corruption, your crime, indeed, your payola.

"We don't need graffiti or ten thousand jails
Or half off (of what price?) at company sales.
We don't need your alcohol, baseball or beer.
So what, may we ask, are you all doing here?

What is the point?

"Globalization is just a big hoax
To enrich the elites, namely most of you folks.
It allows you to pay the most minimal wage
To Third World job seekers and those underage.

"We view with true horror and greatly deplore
The huge growing gap between you and the poor.
Your princes of industry earn, you'll agree,
Considerably more than our whole GNP.

"We've no admiration for crude jingoism,
Heroism, egoism, indeed, any 'ism'.
As for your knowledge of Space savoir faire . . .
No, go back to Texas, you're happier there!"

To distinguished Earth visitors this seemed perverse.
They were the greatest in God's universe.
Chosen, square-jawed, such utter perfection
Now told to retire in a homeward direction?

"Clearly," they muttered, "these dwellers in space
Have heard the wrong stories of Earth's marketplace.
Capitalism sorts the wheat from the chaff."
(If this wasn't so brutal, it might make you laugh.)

"It's the one worldwide system to make wrong things right."
(Provided you're clever and wealthy and white.)
"They don't understand how it makes you feel free
To get juicy cash-backs on your new SUV."

"Ah," said a columnist, "here's an idea.
We've promising real-estate openings here.
They've no military forces or means of protection,
Let's start building brigs for their early detention."

Then most of these Chosen, for all they were worth,
Grabbed what they could of this duplicate Earth.
The water grew grimy, the air made men sick.
The country? Transformed into concrete and brick.

Gas stations sprouted, a fifty-mile mall,
With black-belching trucks to disfigure the sprawl.
The beaches grew dirty and in every stream
Were mercuried salmon and half-poisoned bream.

The natives, sequestered in refugee camps,
Looked bitter and joyless like ill-favoured tramps.
And their children fought back with their sticks and their stones,
Deprived of good food they were just skin and bones.

And the elders all muttered: *What is the point?*

I am sad for these natives and weep for their wrongs
I weep for their laughter, their jokes and their songs.
But I'm slightly conflicted, for in the US
The country has seen an improvement, no less.

The haters of taxes have colonized space,
Leaving behind a more tolerant place.
Despisers of poor people, sour plutocrats
Have abandoned the country like ravenous rats.

Now we have here on Earth a liberal regime,
Where once compromise was a foolish young dream.
I have to admit that I once did suspect
We would never again see such mutual respect.

Now the government serves both the rich and the poor,
And narrow self-interest does not dictate law.
And I pray this regime does not disappoint
And we never need ask again:

What is the point?

CPSIA information can be obtained
at www.ICGtesting.com
Printed in the USA
FSOW01n0307280416
19772FS